MW00783383

111 Days of Divine Intervention

A Mother's Healing Journey

Mary D'Agostino

This book is dedicated to my children, grandchildren, and my ancestors. Healing and blessings to those who have come before me and those who will come after. I write this to remember that we are all held together in divine love, always.

Volume 1

979-8-218-21030-4 ISBN Number

cover photo by Noah Harold

111 Days of Divine Intervention

How to use this book

Opening this book opens a healing portal. Within its pages you will find words of love, inspiration, and hope woven together in story, poetry, and reflections. All are infused with blessings intended to soothe your grieving heart.

Just as there is no right or wrong way to grieve, there is no right or wrong way to use this book. You may use it as a journal, a daybook of inspiration, or a healing companion on your journey through mourning, bereavement, and grief. Use it as a resource of guidance and wisdom to help you through the most difficult of life passages. Use it as a way to connect with your innermost self and experiences past or present that need your loving compassion.

You can use it by opening its pages randomly and reading whatever story or message is on the page before you. You can start at day one and proceed through the book in order. You can use the messages or stories as journaling prompts or pause for reflection. If there is an action offered, you may implement it, if it feels right for you.

When one is in the deep recesses of grief, and all the changes it creates, our bodies and minds may feel heavy, confused, and exhausted. This is when your soul steps up. This book offers sacred healing, peace-filled moments that assure you that your soul is stepping up and stepping in. Use it as a rescue remedy from your soul. The soul is the timeless and eternal part of who you are. Undying, like the love you have for your loved one who is no longer with you in body.

To enter the portal of this book is to have a small amount of belief that grief is a journey and through it you will receive that which you need to heal. Nature, loving gestures, introspection, hope, kindness, and compassion will be your guide.

This book contains sixteen true stories, over one-hundred gentle prompts and a few poems that add up to 111 days of Divine Interventions. Tales of synchronistic moments, simple and miraculous interventions to assist you on your journey through grief. While this is my experience of my journey, I offer my experience as a gift to support you on your journey as well. A shift in perspective, a gentle knowing, and a warm hug for you.

What is a Divine Intervention?

A divine intervention is a very real experience that can be something as big as a birth of a child to something as small as a blooming flower. It is the knowing, albeit mysterious or unexplainable, that you are a part of something grand and profound. It is an unconditionally loving experience that is beyond logic and yet contains physical logic. It connects the mystery of life with the everyday. It can be a gentle jolt, a word, a thought, or experience that defies logic and leaves you changed. It is that which we need when all else fails us and there is no map of how to proceed. It is the unconditional loving friend who puts their arm around your shoulder and says, come, let us explore life over here for a bit. It is the sudden undeniable realization that you are part of something loving and good and that you too are an amazing array of miracles.

These stories of divine interventions are my unquestionably real personal experiences. They are full and rich. They take me to a place of believing and knowing that is beyond doubt. I hope they give you this same knowing and belief to experience your own divine interventions. Divine Interventions are like that. I know that life goes on after death. For me it came through these stories, shared from my perspective. I changed certain names of those involved as to honor their anonymity and the tenderness of their personal experiences.

As you read, feel yourself wrapped in divine love. Feel the worries and concerns flow away for a moment in time as you open gently and imagine what divine intervention might be awaiting your attention.

Day 1

Why 111 Days?

On January 11, 2017, I was given a gift of a guided meditation class entitled Angelic Breath with the Archangels. It was prerecorded so I could listen at my leisure. I did so on that exact day. It turned out the entire experience was profoundly, uniquely designed for me to receive what I needed to support me through the devastating days ahead. A divine intervention that solidified the truth that amidst great loss and disruption, there is indeed the flow of divine grace.

I discovered the positive effects of guided meditation long ago. I find great value in accessing the inner worlds of imagination, for all of life is born of our imaginations. Guided meditation and journaling are both part of my personal practice, as well as tools I use to assist others on the journey of spiritual, mental, emotional, and physical well-being. Messages from the realms of angels, or more simply put, the great love and support that is the foundation of our existence, is available, especially when I quiet my mind and journey within.

This meditation class was about one hour in length, consisted of music and breathing exercises and was created to invoke the archangels Michael and Raphael on the 1/11 day. This day was chosen because it is supposedly a special angel number day. I believe every day can be infused with angelic presence. Angels have been a strong and resilient part of my life since I was a child and have intervened in the most helpful of ways ever since. For me, angels are a most loving presence of pure god essence. So, onward I went expecting a most lovely and blissful meditation.

Earbuds in, recording ready, I relax, listen, and go with the experience by following the prompts of the facilitator. Not long into the meditation, the expected bliss turned uniquely intense, and a bit uncomfortable. I was assured I was safe, and whatever followed was important and I needed to pay attention. A vision along of one archangel on my right, and one on my left appeared. This vision was accompanied by a strong surprising feeling of forceful guidance. I was being pushed forward through two pillars of light into what felt like a tight squeeze on either side. I was focused ahead. The light pillars looked like three ones in a row, with me in the middle of two pushy and a bit intimidating angels on either side. They urged me forward through what seemed a tight and narrow passage.

I trust the angel energy explicitly, so with resistance in tow, I indeed moved forward as instructed. I was feeling that push into something that I was not sure I was ready for, nor did I want. I wrote afterwards in my journal of the experience-

> *The straight and narrow path that looked like 111 is a guide for me. It felt like I was cross country skiing and had to stay within the lines. I am to stay on this pathway. Be deliberate. Listen. Invite in the angels*

at all times. You are not to fit yourself into someone else's version of what you want. Listen and act upon what is right for you.

The healing is here and is activated. I live inside the angels and the angels live inside   me. They will help me with everything.

These words were a combination of my thoughts and feelings, along with the wisdom of my spirit, and angelic guidance. I was greatly moved by this meditation experience and was in a contemplative state for the next few days.

On the evening of Friday January 13, 2017, I was in session with a dear couple who I had the pleasure to work with a few times prior to this evening. It was dark outside and cozy inside my home office space, or what is called my Healing Room. During the session, I had a most intense vision. With my work as healer and medium I often have visions for the client as part of our work together. I shared what I saw with the couple, but it did not seem to belong to them. This has never happened before in session and never since. The vision is as follows.

I saw a large, powerful goddess in the star filled night sky. Red and orange colors swirled about her. She had giant arms that held the entire world. She was reaching down to the earth and placing stars upon the planet. Then she took stars off the planet and placed them back in the sparkling star-filled dark sky. It was a clear and potent vision of what felt like the Mother

Goddess of life and death. She was incredibly loving and beautiful, yet deliberate and concise.

I completed the session, sent the couple home after they did receive the messages and healing they needed. I proceeded to relax before turning in for the evening. I picked up my phone and scrolled through photos of my children, landing on ones of my youngest son Brandon at his 24th birthday celebration that occurred a few months prior. The video showed the sweet and gentle spirit of my son. His toddler nephews, my grandsons, were singing him happy birthday in their joyful voices. My son was beaming with the light of the candles. I smiled at the photo, feeling the essence of such tender love. I touched the phot with my fingers, sweeping a blessing upon them all. A deep and resounding peace settled into my body.

My son Brandon, youngest of my five, faced many challenges over the last ten years. Each time he met with a challenge, he knew he could count on me and his siblings. As we traversed difficult experiences, I held to the faith I would always be there for him in ways that grew our souls. It was a great challenge. I continuously offered him guidance, wisdom, and unconditional love. I learned how to help him through addiction, mental health, and trauma. It was a continuous healing and learning experience. He recently found a spot on his life journey where he was doing well, working at a job he loved selling luxury cars, and living in a new place with a new roommate. I was cautiously optimistic. I found that staying within the present day and taking one day at a time was best for my peace of mind when it came to my son Brandon and his life choices.

About an hour later I fell asleep quickly and slept unusually sound, unaware of the texts and calls that were coming in from his fiancé that evening and early morning. At about 8:30 am on Saturday morning January 14, her frantic calls got through. I answered with a bit of hesitancy.

"Brandon was missing. He took a Maserati sports car from the dealership where he was employed out for a test drive Friday evening around 7:00pm and did not return."

I listened intently. She continued. "He did not answer any of my calls nor show up for a planned date."

No one knew where Brandon was. She asked if I heard from him. I had not.

I immediately went onto his social media account and saw that he posted a self-made live video at about 7:30 pm the prior evening. One hand on the steering wheel, of a brand-new Maserati, his other held the phone focusing on the speedometer as the car accelerated from numerical 2mph to 111mph, and the video ended. I stared at this posting of my son showing the world how fast he was going inside a luxury sports car.

A wave of peace came over me, and then terror as I realized this was posted last evening, the last time anyone saw or heard from him. I waivered back and forth for what seemed like many minutes but was a mere second or two. I knew this video was a direct message to me, from my son. I felt the familiar strength of angels surround me and hold me as I heard a message. "He went through the portal." The portal of three columns of light with angels by my side. The 111 Portal.

I took a deep breath and could feel the energy of my son Brandon. He was telling me something. "I am all right mom! I am ok." Immediately a vision of his face, surrounded by what looked like sparkling water came into my awareness. He was smiling his big, beautiful smile. For that split second, I again felt peaceful. Assured. Then my strong mother instincts took precedence and I needed to know where he was physically.

"If you are ok, where are you?" Again, the vision of his smiling face.

His fiancé had contacted everyone letting us all know he was missing. There was a frantic move by me, his siblings, friends, and dad to find him. He was last seen taking a car from the dealership for a test drive at about 7pm that prior evening. The dealership told us he had not shown up for work that morning and they did not know where he was. Then, they stopped answering our frantic calls. We called hospitals, reached out to all his friends. His brother and best friend went to the places they thought he might be. Nothing. It was the most horrific time of waiting and wondering. Again, I called the angels forth and again I was reassured, he went through the portal. What was this portal? The portal of Light? Could it be? I felt Brandon's energy present with me, but I did not feel that unusual.

Terror of a missing child, known for disappearing into his own addiction and struggle, intertwined with a resounding peace as the day wore on. Finally, in the late afternoon hours we were all called to gather at the sheriff station, a mere mile from where the dealership was located. No information, just that we had to come. It was there we learned the physical details of what I was so divinely guided to prepare for. He did indeed drive that Maserati at a high speed. Maybe it was his hand in the video. The sheriff would not confirm but we knew it was. Brandon was only doing what he must have done many times before. Breaking rules and pushing the edges of life. The road was deserted, dark and the perfect place for a test drive. Yet, this time he was not to make it back home. The edges yielded to him. Instead, it is believed he lost control of the car at the high speed of 111 while trying to maneuver a curve in the road. The vehicle hit the curve and flew 120 feet into the air before landing in a retention pond. This was at the same time I was in session and having the experience of the Goddess of Life and Death, returning the stars from the earth, up into the heavens.

My son died instantly on the eve of January 13, and yes, it was the time I was in session. He was found late that morning, by a runner on the adjacent trail. The car lay hidden on the side of the road. Once he was found, and all went through the channels to identify him, that is when they could notify us, his family. A truly tragic story, yet one I share with hope and healing. One I share so you too know we are so much more than we give ourselves credit for!

As in life, my son's death was surrounded by divine interventions that cannot be explained in any way other than the truth that love lives on past physical death. His life came as a miracle, as all of us do. His soul and my soul knew there would be great tragedy, but we would survive it together. His body would perish, but his presence would remain with me and his loved ones. The soul does not die but is freed from the confines of the body and goes on to experience heaven, or other dimensions of which there are many. There is and always will be a continued relationship with my child who now lives on in Spirit. There are no explanations for the continuous divine interventions other than this truth. I know it in the depths of my being.

My son, Brandon has made it his mission to continue to make sure I know he is always here and that there is so much more to our lives than we may think. We truly are spiritual beings having a human experience.

The portal of 111 did indeed open. I was not warned but rather prepared by my meditation experience two days prior. My soul was readying. An immense buffer of Angelic light remains around me. I would be held amidst the great tragedy and trauma that unfolded like a slow-motion nightmare. I would stay focused, remembering that an angel flanked each one of my sides and that the portal of heaven opened before me to welcome my son. He flew home, through the portal, for it was his time. I could walk him part of the way, then the great love of the big, giant Mother Goddess of the night sky who lovingly places stars upon the earth and takes them back up to their home among the heavens, would usher him the rest of the way.

May She hold you too as you receive the healing balms that are here for you as you read this book. The healing balms will go directly into your heart and soul in the exact way you need it. That is how Divine Interventions work. They leave you with no doubt something of a most miraculous form is indeed at play. It may not make sense to the mind, but the heart knows. The soul awakens and life becomes more expansive. May you be blessed immensely.

Day 2

Today is a day to walk. It can be outdoors or indoors. Each step is a connection of your essence with the essence of the ground below. The ground holds you in good stead.

Day 3

Today is a day to breathe with awareness. Each inhale and each exhale are a miraculous circulation of life force. Even in deep grief, your body is still inviting in life. Today as you breathe, imagine you are inhaling love, and exhaling love.

Day 4

Grief is a natural expression of love. The deeper the love, the deeper the grief. Be assured, the depths of grief will be met with the expansive light of love.

Day 5

Today is a day for non-rushing. What does it feel like to move slowly?

Day 6

Grief causes inner emotional disruption. Like a fussy baby, we aren't easily consoled. What might bring soothing relief today?

Day 7

Look up. What does the sky look like today? Take note.
The sky blesses.

Day 8

Today, meet yourself with compassion. What does compassion have to say today? Maybe compassion tells you that All is Well in some far-reaching corner and that is where you and compassion meet today.

Day 9

Today, meet yourself with kindness. Kindness offers a buffering place within where you can retreat to when the harshness of the world gets too close.

Day 10

What Happened When You Died?

Journal Entry: Wednesday February 22, 2017. Happy half-birthday to me. I feel very tired and too much out there. Too much exposed-too much. Too much with others.

Too exposed. Too raw. Too much. I seek solace and peace today. Small moments of peace and quiet will help me.

It hurts a lot. It hurts so very much. Like ice running through my veins. Prickly.

Help me angels. Today, please help me.

I ask for help in all ways right now. I don't even know how to ask for help or what to ask for. How can I be helped when what has happened is the worse thing possible? Today I want to scream, NO, this can't be so. No. No. No.

It is not ok and never will be. Ever. I ask for help this day, in all ways, through unconditional Love. Thank you.

Then I went on a walk. As I walked my usual route, through the park and onto the path that curves through a place hidden from view, I decided to converse with Brandon. I do like this part of my walk. It is quiet, graced with a small creek on one side, spindly trees, winter bare bushes, and a waist high stone wall on the other. It is here I feel connected and safe. I am relieved to be moving my body and feeling a sense of my own self, shaky but also sure as I step on my familiar path.

Since the very day Brandon transitioned, I continue to hear him clearly in my mind. We converse often, just as you would do so with anyone as if they were right next to you. He also respects my need for my own healing and privacy. This time, he asked me if I really wanted to know what happened when he died. I wasn't too shocked with the question, for I did wonder more on the subject. I needed to know that he did not suffer. As a medium, many of the people in spirit that I bring through need to let their loved ones know they did not suffer. We need to know they did not suffer. It is also something we can't make up or make true if it is not. I decided to trust my son with whatever information he needed to give to me at that most tender time.

This day was less than two months since his passing, and as much as I was held in healing love by my extraordinary experiences with the 111 Portal, the questions regarding his suffering would rage around in my mind like hot embers.

When I heard him pose the question this day, I quickly answered. "Yes, I want to know. But please spare me any details that would upset me." I am apt to speak with my son as I would if he was physically walking beside me. I suggest you do the same when you speak with your loved ones in spirit. They are still them. Maybe a bit 'more them' than ever! They don't become all knowing or judgmental. Quite the contrary.

It is usually their mission to remind you of that which is most important.

He heartily agreed. I then asked if he could wait until I got home. I wanted to write down what he told me. I felt it of the utmost importance. I walked home, very fast. I took out my journal, sat on my couch and was ready.

"Tell me what happened when you died." I bravely stated. Here is what he answered.

So, here is how it went—I was driving, and along came this giant angel. She snatched me right out of that car. She lifted me up and held me in her arms—I thought it was you Mom—I thought it was you. She looked and smelled like you. She felt like you—like I was going home. She held me and we watched the car—just for a moment and she took me somewhere. She held me and told me how much she loved me—I still thought it was you mom—I think it was you. I felt the connection—like when you love me, that Love goes on and on and on. She was your love and my love and all the love that I ever felt and all the Love I ever gave. I felt this warm glow and it was—IS where I have been returning to over and over and over again. I remove myself from it and I visit places and then I return to the love. I really can't leave it. Ever. It was all a part of the plan—to light up this Love again. In our family—make it —the love, the strongest. More like remembrance. We forgot. You didn't forget Mom— you never forgot Love. You fed me Love Mom—so much Love. Thank you Mom.

Thank you, Brandon.

Now I want you to be fed love, Mom—over and over. Your angel is telling me to tell you that. Over and over, Mom you are being fed love. Loved.

It all started coming together again. My experiences since January 11 through this profound message on February 22 were solidifying the divine interventions. Weaving them together to tell the story of my son's soul and my part in his journey. I was shown the portal from earth to the dimensions one travels in death. I was shown it on 1/11. I went into the portal but could not go further or through. I waited in the portal from 1/11 until 1/13 when I saw the giant Mother (angel) Goddess pick up the stars and place them in heaven. I helped usher my son Brandon through.

When a mother gives birth, she is the portal through which a child enters life. Her body is the portal. I ushered Brandon through my body and into his life. I had the great honor to usher him through the portal of divine light out of his body and into the spirit realms. He called it the arms of the angel or the Mother who he knew as me. My life-long studies and remembering of my wisdom and ancestral knowledge of soul, life, death, and birth all prepared me for my leading part in my son Brandon's life. Or shall I say our parts in each other's lives.

You see, Brandon came to me as an answer to a prayer. Much like the one I wrote at the beginning of the day on February 22, 2017. I called out to the divine to help me somehow, someway. It was late in 1991 and I did not know how I would be able to continue in the life I was living. I needed a divine intervention. In 1990 my family of four kids, a husband, a dog, and cat, moved from my home of thirty years. We left my big extended family in California and went off to Massachusetts. I left everyone and everything I knew behind. I was deep in the throes of a dysfunctional marriage and living isolated in a new place that was very different from the one I left. So, I prayed for a divine intervention. Something needed to happen. My husband was increasingly hostile, and my family and friends were so far away. New friendships were blossoming, I was trying hard to be the best mom, wife, and person, but I felt so very alone. Four kids, a newborn, a toddler with medical needs, so much responsibility, so little support.

And then I was surprisingly pregnant with Brandon. Not that this would be easy by any means, but something changed in me. I could only focus on immediate needs, my health, and my kids. One new friend became my constant companion and later Brandon's god mother. Brandon came in from the heavens as a divine intervention. He brought me the change I was asking for. This new little life would change everything. I knew not how, but it did happen. Soon we were moving again, and life took a turn for the better. For a little while at least. He was the answer to my prayer. I am the answer to his. We remember Love.

Through Brandon's untimely entrance and untimely passing I am shown the larger picture. We have known each other throughout time and space. Our lives intertwine like the feelings of great loss and great spiritual truths intertwine throughout my days.

I will always wonder if I could have done something to save him. I will always crave a physical hug from my boy and to see him one more time. And I will still occasionally wonder if he suffered in the accident. Almost in the same nanosecond of the thoughts, I receive the peace of knowing what he told me on that chilly February day in 2017. That knowing brings a peace that continuously helps me heal. For as a mother is the portal through which a child enters life, she is also eternally a part of the child as the child is a part of her. Cells connect us. Cells and soul. Remember love and as that is remembered the healing can reach beyond the physical and set afire the path of healing from one realm to the next.

Day 11

Today converse with your loved one in spirit. Ask questions. Whatsoever is on your heart and mind. If you hear anything but love, that is not your loved one, it is your grief or guilt. Ask from your heart. Listen from your heart. Only love.

Day 12

There is no right or wrong way to grieve. Today, meet yourself with nonjudgment.

Day 13

Today reflect on your soul journey. What if birth and death were just different sides of the same coin? What if where we come from when we are born and where we go to when we die are the same place? It is a place of pure Love.

Day 14

Remembering love means taking really good care of yourself. I was trained to always ask "what do *you* need." At times what I need is to tend to others. At times, I couldn't lift a finger to tend, if I tried. Ask yourself - What might I need today?

Day 15

Remembering love means taking care of your body. Today is a day to pay attention to your body and take one simple step to help your body feel better.

Day 16

Remembering love means giving space to the sadness.
Today is a designated safe space for the deep sadness.

Day 17

Remembering love means to let the easy feelings co-exist with the hard ones. Today it is ok, normal, and healthy to laugh.

Day 18

Today, it's all about salt baths, massages, and body gentleness. Pampering is on order today.

Day 19

Remembering love means remembering that the best things are often the simplest. Rest, food, and water. Keep it simple.

Day 20

The Miracle of the White Feather

Mother's Day, 2017, was a mere four months after Brandon's passing. Realizing how long it takes to process all those divine interventions along with all the sadness of experiencing the death loss of my child is a part of my reality now. But that first year seems like time out of time. It feels like birthing a new way of being in a world where one of my beloved children is not physically present. Yes, there were days of deep connection and yes there were days of deep sadness.

Even thinking of that day, Mother's Day, made me incredibly sad. This is a day that celebrated mothering/mothers and all I could think of was that one of my children is no longer living. How could I face the day? Along with the deep sadness was a feeling I am not too familiar with. An inability to push through. Remembering that I was learning a new way of being in this world. Not a new identity. I was and always will be a mom, but how does one go about life when one of my beloved children was no longer here?

Oh, I just wanted to pretend none of these stupid holidays existed anyways. This is where I throw my hands up in surrender and ask for divine interventions. I needed them now!

I don't remember exactly how it came about, but my kids suggested a simple picnic in my backyard. They would take care of it all. I think of how lucky I am to have grown children who were all tending to their grief and trauma too but offered to come together on such a sad day. Greif is exhausting. Each one of my children devastated in their own ways.

They show up with the goodies. Picnic food, sandwiches, salads. I set up tables in the yard. Brandon's two best friends came. They call me Mom. My kids, grandkids and my daughter who lives on the east coast via facetime were all present. The day is a beautiful spring Colorado day.

The food is served, I sit at the round table with my daughter's-in- love (what I call the wives of my sons), and a few of my little grandsons. The young men are seated at a long white picnic table a few feet away, facing me. I can see all my kids today. We eat, quietly, which is not a usual way for us to be. It is usually loud and raucous. I think of Brandon and his absence overwhelms me. Sadness comes and tears start to fall as I look at my kids. They stare at me, wondering if the dam is going to burst. A moment of shared grief, waiting on the precipice of big, overwhelming feelings. Time stops for a moment as we look at each other.

"Ma!" exclaims my Christi. She is sitting directly across from me and starts pointing to something above my head.

"What?" I whisper, a bit thankful the moment broke on the side of relief.

Raeden gets up and walks behind me. She picks something off my shoulder and hands it to me. "This just fell from the sky. We all saw it." She says nonchalantly and walks back to her seat at the table.

What she handed me was a tiny white feather. It fell from a cloudless, treeless, bird- less sky and landed on my shoulder in the exact moment I was thinking about Brandon and wishing he were here. I held the feather out for all to see. My kids and grandkids stare at me, eyes wide, tears flow, heads shake and smiles appear from ear to ear.

"You can't make this sh$%&t up." I say loudly.

Everyone agrees. We continue to eat our Mother's Day meal, with a heavy load off our minds. Somehow, our Brandon has figured out how to join the party and make himself known. He gave me the best mother's day present for my grieving heart.

Day 21

Today ask for a sign from your loved one who has
passed. Be pleasantly surprised. The simple step of
asking connects us heart to heart. This is healing.

Day 22

Brandon's celebration of life service was on January 22, 2017. Close to 500 in attendance. The event center that we chose had tall windows that gave a magnificent view of the Rocky Mountains. Kids, grandkids, and I tucked into a very tacky party limousine to ride together to the service. It was a surreal and solemn experience. There amidst the running lights and spilled champagne smell was some of the most amazing love imaginable. My three sons, my daughter, me, and my grandkids all with tear streaked, wide eyed, broken hearts had no words for each other that would even begin to mend our shattered lives. We drove the scenic route, not wanting to rush the inevitable. As we drove, I stared out the foggy window and saw the barren winter farmland. There in the middle of the field was a giant bald eagle. Standing on the ground, poking around at something he caught for a midday meal. I felt a rush of my son's spirit flow through the limo. He was there, letting us know that as we all showed up for a most horrendous and trying experience there is a comfort in knowing life goes on. Nature does its thing. Life will go on, and now we had to do our thing. Heal.

"Let's get there now." I said to the driver. I did not wish to spend one more moment driving. We sped to the place I would conduct the celebration of my child's life.

As we approached the venue, cars lined the road, the parking lot overflowed. People walked slowly up the hill ascending to pay their respects to us, to me, and to my son. So many people! We parked in the round drive and were escorted in, avoiding cameras and any sign of the media. We went to the small room usually reserved for the bride and her attendees to ready for weddings. Not today. This room would be where the littlest attendees could hang out during the service. Snacks and juice boxes for their hungry tummy's. Silly cartoons on repeat, making upbeat sounds as if this were the most normal day. Little children who would grow up and not remember this day. We would.

I shored my reserves to face the task ahead. I was the only one I trusted to honor my son's life. I would lead the celebration service. It was a fight with his father to agree to a celebration that truly honored how Brandon lived. I made it happen. A divine intervention indeed. I would not have strangers say words about a god my child did not believe in. I would not have strangers saying words of comfort to my family, my friends and Brandon's community. I would do so. In my way. Brandon urged me on.

Brandon lived love alive. I stood my ground. Two dear women friends stood on each side of me, holding me steady like the shining columns of light from the angel's message of 111. They took my arms as I took my place in front of the hundreds of forlorn faces staring my way. I don't remember what I said exactly. I remember I said to hug each other a lot and say I love you often. I led them all in the *Hail Mary*. The prayer from my childhood religion that held the most honor for the divine Mother was an appropriate one for Her presence was mighty on that day in that place high atop a hill overlooking the Rocky Mountains. Within me and within the group gathered the mother goddess's unconditional love was fueled. She was there holding me steady as person after person shared incredible stories of my son. He was a true hero and lover of life. He changed lives, made friends, and never let anyone leave his presence without feeling better. That was my son. That is my son.

The eagle, the divine mother, good people, and a mother's love undenied was how I met myself on that day. All majestic in their own ways, companions to the angels that would guide me forth, reminding that all is well. All is eternally well.

Day 23

Today is a day to honor your bravery. What have you done for yourself during your grief that you may not realize is brave? Today give yourself credit where it is due.

Day 24

Today, I meet myself with loving self-acceptance. A good thing to do each day. Write this down and post it where you can see it every day.

Day 25

Today reflect on what divine intervention means to me. Today ask for a divine intervention.

Day 26

Today, connect with your Higher Power and write a few words about the experience. What name do you give to this experience today?

Day 27

Loss and grief bring destruction. What was, no longer is. Today there is no rush to re-build, instead let the rubble be steppingstones. Careful steps.

Day 28

Everyone needs a place where they feel safe and can rest assured as they heal. Today create a safe nest for yourself.

Day 29

Today notice color. What colors catch your eye? What colors feel soothing today?

Day 30

My broken heart weaved back together into a beautiful mosaic of light, color, and healing love that reaches far beyond the everyday world. Pieces of my heart are with my son beyond the veil. Pieces are within the veil, for the veil is simply a garment that holds together the physical and spiritual realms. Together. Not separate. Pieces of my heart are with the mothers and fathers in my ancestral lineage who also lost children. Pieces of my heart are in the tears shed, the ground I walk, the meals made, the work I do, the gardens planted and with the children and grandchildren of my life. Pieces of my heart are shared here within the pages of this book. Pieces of my heart are with every prayer, every word, every minute, every hour, every day, and every blessing I have lived. Pieces of my heart are within each Divine Intervention that has come to save my life and remind me that love never dies, and we are here to remember love.

Day 31

Grieving is Weaving

I weave stories

I weave words into healing stories.

I weave healings.

I weave energy into healing balms.

I weave wisdom into pearls of beauty shimmering

sparkling in the depths of a dark sea.

I weave my broken open heart together

with love, healing stories, healing balms

creating rainbow light and strands of essence and love.

My broken heart is now a web of colors, fibers of light, stardust,

electric currents of pure potent source energy

connecting broken hearts in the sea of the one heart.

Grieving is weaving.

Day 32

Today is a day to meditate. Beginner or seasoned pro.

How? However, feels good. Easy is best. One way is to set a timer for ten minutes, close your eyes and breathe. Slowly inhale and exhale counting to four each time. Let your mind wander and thoughts drift like the clouds.

Day 33

Today is a day to believe in angels. The big, giant light beings that can shrink to sit on your bed or follow you around the house.

Ask for angels to be made known to you.

Day 34

Today the angels visit again. They are here to help.
How might they help today?

Day 35

Loss and grief bring destruction. What was, no longer is. Today there is no rush to re-build, instead let the rubble be steppingstones. Careful steps.

Day 36

Today invoke self- compassion. Compassion is an art to be practiced.

Day 37

What small and simple joy is on the agenda for today? Putting joy on the agenda is helpful for a mind that gets easily cluttered with grief.

Day 38

Today find a song you remember from childhood or pick a song at random from your playlist. Listen as if it's a message from your loved one in spirit.

Day 39

Emotional support is vital as you grieve. Who or what is emotionally supportive? Set up a system of emotional support. One you can rely on regularly.

Day 40

Brandon's First Birthday in Spirit

Keeping count and track of your life gives meaning and value to the fleeting moments. We count days of the week, months, and years. We keep track of first days, last days, beginnings, middle and ends of days. We ritualize special days with ceremony. Oftentimes without really understanding what we are doing.

Experiencing the death of my son made me acutely aware of how ritualizing the passing of time helped me in my grief. Dates and numbers all meant something, and I found this soothing. As his mother, I was always the keeper of time. His time, my time, our family time, my work, his school, his health. Every moment of his life from the moment I knew I was pregnant with him was in some way mine to keep track of. Even when he no longer lived with me, and he was off in the world, living and keeping his own time, I still was and always would be the original keeper of time for him.

His passing was no different. I would remain the keeper of time for him always. It was my duty and obligation to keep track and make sure his passing was given the proper ceremony and ritual. It was important to continue to honor the day of his birth. At first it was the days that were marked, then the months, and then about nine months in, it was his first birthday without him. The dreaded first.

I had no idea that my role as timekeeper and life tracker of my son would continue once he was in spirit. I did not ever fathom that it would still be important for me to carry this honor. I did not realize how incredibly difficult and undeniably helpful this duty would be and how much fortitude, courage and strength would be called forth. I soon realized that to do so would lend itself to my own healing and show me continuous divine interventions, ones set in place before he was physically born.

Keeping track, is a ritual and ceremony conducive to life. It gives deep meaning to the human experience. I came to this naturally, drawn as I was to the art of ceremony and ritual from my early days. From family meals, daily chores, bedtime stories. From early childhood Friday evening visits and Sunday dinners with my grandparents. From baptisms, weekly church, communion, confirmation and all the rest of the sacraments of my early religious training to family birthdays in a family of eight siblings. It was my duty since I could reach the stove, to bake the birthday cakes and decorate them for each sibling. Ritual and ceremony give form to life.

I taught my children different rituals. We always celebrated birthdays. I made their favorite meals, with their favorite candle lit cake, cupcakes, or cookies for school friends. We made our lives meaningful in simple and meaningful ways. Every day is an opportunity to celebrate the life we live, no matter what frame of mind may be present. I adhered by this then and now.

How would I honor, ritualize, and give ceremony to the day I gave birth to my child twenty-five years prior? The same child who died tragically nine months earlier. What would this day require of me? My grief counselor suggested it be a day for me to do whatsoever I needed. She suggested I think about how I might wish to spend the day. I so appreciated her naming this for me because I did not realize what might be asked of me emotionally as this day approached. I did not realize that this day would have to be for me. I would be tending to myself, both in celebration of the day I gave birth to my child, and in the emotional turmoil that ensued. Anxiety mounted, so I made a plan to take very good care of me.

I would get a massage from my trusted healer on his exact birthday. She met me where I was so many times during those early days. Greif made my body ache deeply. Deeper than I could imagine and, on the day, marking the twenty-five-year anniversary of my son's birth, my body was feeling the loss. My body created him, held him, and birthed him. It ached deeply for him now. Pieces of me disappeared from the planet when he went through that portal. Yes, he lived on, but I felt the loss in my aching mother body. It is a primal instinct to call out to our children and have our bodies search for them when they are no longer here on the planet. Oh, how I needed her light touch and energy healing on this day.

The morning before my massage, I thought about my Brandon, his loves, and his beautiful smile. How might I honor him? What would he like? He was very much into doing Fitness Challenges. A thought came to me. I will do a 90-day Soul Challenge and engage my clients and friends in what was sure to be an empowering experience. It was a great idea, and I could feel my son's spirit agreeing. As I lay on the massage table, the tears started to flow. The table held me as I sobbed and released my grief. My tears were honored. They honored my son. They honored me. After a while my thoughts drifted back to the idea of the 90-day Soul Challenge. Something wasn't quite right about that. Was I not up for it? Was it the name? What was the resistance? I felt my son's lively soul and I heard him say, "Mom, it needs to be the 111 Day Challenge. Think about it Mom. How many days are there between the day of my birth and the day of my death?" I furiously started counting. Laying on the massage table with my body grieving, at the hands of a Master Masseuse and Reiki practitioner, I was a puddle of mind mush. I tried to count the exact days, and I knew it was close but…but…Then I heard Brandon again. "Mom, wait until you are done here." So, I did. And as I sat at my favorite sandwich place afterwards, I got out my phone calendar and counted. Sure enough. It is 111 days between his birthday and the day he transitioned. Exactly.

Now I see that time as the most sacred time of my year. Those days start in very early autumn into early winter. A time to slow down and become more attuned to my inner worlds. I use those 111 days as a way to be in my own Soul Challenge. I turn within, I give myself time to process and I tend to my needs. It is a very special time and again, I know without a doubt that this is a Divine Intervention. It is exactly what I need to not only know my son lives on, but that there is a higher purpose and a plan that is beyond my comprehension, but exactly attuned to my most precious needs.

A true miracle.

Day 41

Today seek connection for your broken heart. Gentle, inspiring connection heals a broken heart.

Day 42

I often connect first thing in the morning as I open my eyes. I say to myself and God/Universe/Powers that be, "thank you for this beautiful day".

How might you greet your day that your day will bring a shift in energy?

Day 43

Today, remember that gentle shifts count. Today take a different route while driving or walking and see what happens.

Day 44

Brandon Grows Angel Wings

For Christmas, just before the second-year anniversary of Brandon's passing, my son Tom gave me and each of his siblings an enlarged photo of Brandon, beautifully framed. The photo appears on the cover of this book. It was taken by Brandon's best friend Noah. Brandon was recovering from a near death experience about eighteen months before his actual passing. He went to live under the care and watchful eye of his brother Alex and Brandon was indeed on the road to recovering.

He was on his own soul healing journey. The story of the photo goes like this- He picked up a large log with Noah's help hoisted it upon his shoulders and carried it down the train tracks. He was showing his physical, mental, emotional, and spiritual strength. This is a most precious gift. I did not know this photo existed. I learned that Brandon walked the train tracks every day and journaled too! I promptly placed this precious photo atop a bookshelf in my living room. A place of honor.

Approaching the second anniversary of Brandon's passing I sat in my living room as I do each morning. I start my days in this sunny, bright place. I meditate and do my version of praying. I drink my coffee and write in my journal. It is a holy practice I have been doing for many years. In the recovery years following

Brandon's passing, this ritual took on new life as it was always lifesaving, now it was also a companion in my grief.

On this particular morning as I sat with eyes closed, I heard an urging from Brandon to open my eyes. Needless to say, my son does not always interrupt my morning time. He is also not always invited. It is my time. But as I am apt to do, I listened and followed his cue. I glanced to my right towards the photo. To my surprise I saw a bright light appear on the photo as if he sprouted a wing. I gasped. I picked up my phone and as I leaned just a bit forward two angel wings appeared on his back. I took a moment to photograph this beautiful miracle. The light shone in exactly the right way on this photo of Brandon to show me he sprouted angel wings.

He may not have been able to stay on this earth, but he indeed has the heart of an angel and is staying around for all of us to know it is so!

Day 45

Recovery is a word we often associate with a negative connotation. What if tending to our grief is a recovery process. We are recovering from loss. And recovering ourselves.

Day 46

What if as you traverse the days of bereavement and grief you are recovering something beautiful and important? Recovering the love. Recovering the memories.

Day 47

You can continue your relationship with your loved one in spirit. How might you like to do so?

Day 48

It is healthy to talk frequently to your loved one in spirit. It is also healthy to continue your relationship with your loved one in Spirit.

Day 49

Today is the day you find a miracle in an unlikely place.

Day 50

Finding the Owl Feather

I love owls. The owl art of the 1970's always spoke to me. The big eyes, the knowing looks. Of course, these were cartoon type owls. Not real. But remember, your spirit speaks to you very personally and shows itself to you in ways that make sense to you. Owls held intrigue and wisdom. The wise old owl was a positive expression.

When I was a young woman of twenty-four, the age Brandon was when he left his physical body, I was deeply engaged in my life of raising two little children. I was a single mom, working, growing, playing, and healing. I was on a spiritual journey too, having had a spiritual awakening when my daughter was born and then again at age twenty-two.

I was asked to participate in a three-day retreat that was created and being facilitated by a friend who was just learning more about his indigenous ancestry. I wished to support him in this venture, but being raised mostly disconnected from my indigenous ancestry, I knew nothing about what this retreat might hold other than it was a way to relax, meditate, eat healthy meals and be in a beautiful place in nature. Somehow, I managed child-care, time off work and away I went.

The retreat was in a small town in Northern California, known for its hot springs. No coffee, no alcohol, no outside interference. That was kind of nice. This was also back in the day of land lines only, bulky answering machines and no computers. Yes, we still needed to decompress and detach from daily distractions! My friend led us on what he called journey meditations. We soaked in 'clothing optional' hot springs. What a freeing experience this was. I found it life changing. No pretense, no judgments, just people "baring their skin and soul." I remained open and curious and cautious. I knew that to open oneself to the spiritual worlds within and around required a deeper level of self-respect and respect of the spirits. How did I know this? Perhaps my ancestors were with me!

On the last evening, we gathered outside in a circle. Dusk settling in, my friend started drumming, telling us that we were now doing something to invoke spirits. I was not feeling very comfortable with this. Again, my intuition and wisdom kicked in. I intuitively knew that without a good solid foundation of knowledge and expertise, invoking spirits might not be such a good idea. Summoning spirits should not be done with a laze faire attitude. Looking back, I realize I was feeling all the energies of the land, the people gathered, and all the spirits being called forth. My friend, the leader was respectful, yet I didn't quite trust him, after all we were kind of his guinea pigs in his just opened connection with and guidance from his ancestral spirit helpers. He might be going where he was not yet ready.

I left the group and sat on a hill a short way outside the circle of spirit conjuring. A safe distance. This took courage, for I did not wish to disrespect my friend, yet it was imperative I remove myself. Again, I never participated in anything like this before, but inherently knew if I was to even attempt to walk among the spirit worlds, I would need distance and boundaries from whatever they were doing here. To my surprise, another member of the group was doing the same. She sat quietly amidst the scrub brush. We exchanged knowing looks. I briefly shared my feelings. "Not sure what he's doing. Not sure this is right." She nodded in agreement.

I listened to the drumming and relaxed into the quite evening. I was lulled by the sky full of stars and the company of a kindred cautious friend. I closed my eyes for a moment, feeling held and safe. And there it was! Flashing in my mind's eye was a bright blue neon owl. Big eyes. A knowing look. What was this? The drumming stopped. Our group was called together to share. My outlier friend and I joined back in. People shared experiences of meeting their spirit animal. I did not remember hearing that term, nor asking to meet an animal in this drumming meditation. I was resisting, tending to my own well-being, but it was there as clear as day in the dark of the night. A big flashing neon blue cartoon-like, bird of wisdom.

I didn't share my experience with the group. I kept my spirit animal to myself for many years to come. As I returned home and back into my daily life, I did notice all the owls nearby. Owl paintings, owl macrame, owl jewelry. People gave me owl gifts since I was a little girl. But did I ever even see a live owl? No, I only heard them occasionally hooting in my suburban neighborhood. They remained mysterious and elusive.

Fast forward twenty years. I returned full force to my spiritual journey to support me as I went through a tumultuous divorce. The owl started showing up again. They appeared on the photo of me, taken in Athens Greece on the wall of the Acropolis ruins. Around my feet orbs of light that looked like owl faces with big bright eyes were captured on film. It was the only photo of the roll that had these orbs, so I know they were my owl spirit. Athena is the Goddess who watches over the city of Athens and has an owl on her shoulder to help her see all and there I was, sitting at her temple and the owls were gathering in spirit once more. My ancestors are from Italy and Greece, Western Europe, Africa and the Huron-Wendat peoples.

Owl is my original spirit helper. I know this now. It is always with me. I am aware of its power, protection and messages of stealth movement, fierce awareness, and strength. I have learned to allow it to help me see what is hidden, albeit painful, and to make my move only when I am ready. Owl helps me gain clarity and wisdom in the dark. It is there to help me see where I may be deceiving myself or where others wish to deceive me.

The owl in all its ancient wisdom has helped me through many a devastating challenges, change, losses, and gains. It is always there since it showed itself in fancy neon blue flashy, energy. Despite my resistance that animal spirit shows up for me. Always. As needed.

Fast forward another fourteen years and it is now five months into the time after the death of Brandon. I was deeply mourning and grieving. I gave myself lots of time to do so, for the early stages after death loss are a crucial recovery time. I knew if I did not take it slow, I would never recover. I had to apply everything I had learned thus far and more. Unfortunately, the people I thought would or should understand the greatest loss a person could face, did not. There was a lot of denial of pain and a lot of 'get on with it'. This was mighty hurtful. The sting of words and attitudes of those steeped in a culture of denial and misunderstanding of the power of grief cut me deeply. Our culture does not know how to grieve. It is something not talked about, pushed under the rug, and deeply criticized. My family of origin did not let grief open their hearts. This is what hurt most. The cold and uncaring acts by others telling me to forget or move on were like sharp steel traps that dared me to stay away or risk grave injury to my body, mind, and spirit.

We all will die from these bodies. We all have much to learn about life and death and soul and love. Even then, in the early times of my loss I knew that grief can be a friend that helps us become more human, more alive while here and incredibly more kind, patient and loving. Life kicks everyone's butts. No one escapes it alive. But I do not wish to escape. I have my owl companion always guiding me to go deeper into the darkness and it will protect me, like my angels have always done. And now my son Brandon is a guide too. A strong young man with angel wings. I am so very grateful my indigenous ancestral roots had grown strong over the years. I know better. I know grief and mourning as life-giving and ever so healing.

It was during this early time of five months past Brandon's transition that several family of origin members, decided it was a good time to have a family reunion. They expected me to travel 1200 miles at a time when I could barely leave my house to visit the grocery store. They pushed and prodded and expected my children and I to leave our safe spaces and show up for a photo op of a family reunion of people who have no idea how to create, maintain or inhabit safe emotional space. My family of origin and I did not spend much time together during the last ten years. I was actively creating my life as an emotionally, mentally, spiritually, and physically safe healing place and to do so I unfortunately had to have clear boundaries around my interactions with them. But still they prodded, pushed, and could not fathom why I wouldn't want to spend a lot of money, time, and energy to pretend to be anything but disappointed in my own families lack of compassion for the greatest pain and loss my children and I were experiencing.

My son in Spirit spoke loudly to me about all of this. I kept my connection with my family as cordial as I could for my grown children's sake, but I could not in any way get myself to go there. Brandon encouraged me to up my game on self-care, self-respect and do what I needed for myself. I literally could not imagine how I would ever be able to make myself pack and plan and leave my safe haven of a home. It was an impossibility. My body reacted by giving me an acute side-ache. Then my knee became swollen, my back rigid and sore. I would not be able to travel. Brandon supported me in my healthy decisions (something I said to him in life so often- "make healthy choices") by showering me with little white feathers, 111 sightings everywhere, flashing lights, and other, otherworldly phenomenon. As did my Owl animal spirit.

I did not attend the reunion, much to those people's dismay. I held firm to my need for alone time and true healing. A dear friend came to visit on that exact weekend. She was one of the friends who stood beside me as I led Brandon's Celebration of Life Ceremony. We decided to take a short-day trip into the mountains and visit Shambala Center. This center is an hour drive, a peaceful retreat filled with the compassion and love of the Buddhist tradition. I visited the center with my children in the past. In fact, my son Alex went a few months prior, leaving prayers and trinkets in honor of Brandon.

My dear friend would care for me by driving, having snacks and resting when needed. She even rented a car for the trip. She pre-ordered and pre-paid for a small four door vehicle. When she went to pick up her rental, they had no car available as promised and she ended up waiting a few hours until one returned. It was not a car though; it was a massive 4by4 truck. It would have to do. We could barely reach the stoop to hoist ourselves into the truck. We fit right in though, driving through the Poudre Canyon in our truck. Big, bold, protective energy. Do not hide your grief. Grieving is big, bold, and often messy. Grieving must be done on your own terms.

The trip up the mountain pass was pleasant. Driving the short distance felt like leaving the heaviness behind and entering into a soothing space of open-hearted kindness. The place is truly magical. Tucked in the mountains, it holds a deep reverence and compassion. Each time I go I feel as if the earth energy there is so happy that it looks like everything was carefully arranged by fairies. The aspen leaves tinkled in the breeze, their eyes giving me a knowing look. The gentle wind brushed away the depths of despair and the wildflowers danced in delight. The people we met along the pathways smiled softly. I felt seen and held in a calm, restful beauty.

Visitors are encouraged to leave tokens of offerings and trinkets in places designated for such along the pathway to the stupa. I stopped to leave an offering for Brandon and found one of his business cards and a few shiny pennies. Alex must have left this on his visit. Spirit smiled and soothed me, holding me in my grief. Although the grounds keepers I met along the path did not know why I was there, I felt their kindness as a strong flowing energy, holding and nourishing my broken heart. I felt the spirit of many animals, the ground, the trees, and the flowing breeze. My soul was acknowledging me for doing that which brought healing and for seeking sacred and safe spaces for myself. Everything there was acknowledging me with a gentle nod and a warm and beautiful day. I was held in the soul of place. This place had a great big soul!

The most perfect day concluded when we returned to the truck. I fumbled with a small bottle of sunscreen and the cap fell into the deep crevices between the seats. I stuck my hand down and tried to feel for the cap, but to no avail. It was lost somewhere under the seats for sure. I opened my door and carefully jumped down and out of the truck to get a better view. The cab of the truck waist high! I looked under the seat and saw something that did not look like a bottle cap. I felt around to see if I could get it. I reached my hand farther under my seat and pulled out a great horned owl wing feather. A rush of the deepest healing energy flowed through my body. I held up the feather for my friend to see. She gasped.

"Where did you get that?" she asked.

"Under my seat." I answered.

We stared at each other in amazement. Sheer surprise, but also wise knowing.

How did the feather get under the seat of the truck we were not supposed to have? So much had to conspire on my behalf for me to find this owl feather at this exact time in this exact place, on this exact day. I made a wise healing choice.

I kept the feather. It speaks to me often reminding me that life is always conspiring on my behalf. When I tend to myself in ways that bring me healing love, safe spaces, self-respect, self-regard, and use my power and light in service to love, I am going to be all right.

It is an incredibly brave thing to go against a family of origin and a culture that tells one how to grieve in ways that do not feel authentic or healing. It is incredibly brave to trust one's knowing, to find your true way, and to be open to that which feels right to you. Especially when those in your life who held places of power have steered you otherwise for reasons that are not helpful or beneficial.

One of my spirit animals is indeed the owl. It protects and reminds me of my hidden power. The owl helps me to know when it is time to go within, retreat, and connect with my internal knowing, wisdom, and divinity. When I need to be made aware of the deceptive nature of those who are around me, to be shown hidden truths, the owl shows up. When I need to remember, bring forth and trust my superpowers of knowing and wisdom, the owl shows up. When I need to allow death, endings, and completion to share with me its medicine, owl shows up. The owl has been with me many a year now, helping me in its own quiet, but potent ways. I have learned much under its watchful neon eyes and tutelage.

When we follow the wisdom of our hearts, the knowing that we carry within grows. When our knowing grows, we are able to take care of ourselves and others in ways that truly are healing and regenerative. And don't worry, your spirit helpers will show up in the exact right way, at the exact right times for you.

Day 51

What animals do you have a kindred connection with? These could be animals in the wild, domesticated, or tamed. What animals are your companions?

Day 52

Do certain animals speak to you? Today listen and imagine what they might be saying.

Day 53

Synchronicities abound. Today take notice the
synchronicities you encounter.

synchronicities- (webster's definition) the coincidental
occurrence of events that seem related but are not explained
by conventional mechanisms of causality.

Day 54

In grief, we are stretched and broken open. This leaves us adrift, yes but it also gives room for a deeper healing from places that we may not have noticed before. Today be open for something that may have formerly escaped your view.

Day 55

Poetry for 111 Days

I have written poetry since I was a young teen. I wrote it to express deep feelings that could not be expressed any other way. I find poetry a dance with words. Emotion poured into thought, creating a string of words that give meaning to the heaviest of feeling. My poetry helps me understand when meaning alludes or is hidden in the very words I write.

During my mourning time I sought counsel at the local Hospice Center. There I was met with artists and therapists and healing balms of the most perfect sort for me. I attended monthly art journaling and art therapy group. It was here I found communion. The way art can hold and allow like no other in times of devastation was brought forth for me, from me and around me.

I made simple art, wrote poetry, and was tended to among others. It was here that I was supported in my unique journey, met with compassion, knowledge, and support. I was encouraged to do that which felt right for me, allowed to listen, or be in silence, offered "interventions" or ways to pour forth a grief so horrific there was no other way than to surround it with my essence and see it on its way with words.

These are two poems I wrote. The first is an homage to three years of mourning. It was the third December, the third year, an anniversary of this trilogy of grieving. I thought this a great feat of accomplishment. I survived the first three years post death of my son. I not only survived but I was receiving healing, getting the needs of my broken open heart met little by little. I was coming through a portal of both light and darkness. I wrote of this upcoming anniversary of three Decembers in my journal. I then attended Art Therapy Group. We were shown an art technique using old books, a black marker, and magazine clippings.

As I searched the boxes of images cut from old magazines, I saw the exact words I wrote about in my journal that morning. *Three Decembers.* The chill ran through my body as I picked up the words. I found pages from an old book as instructed and began to create a poem. I darkened words and left a few alive. A dance of dark and light, with words. Like life, I can only make of it what I will. I cannot ask for a life void of pain. I only wish to heal from the devastation of pain. So, I shall use this intervention to write poetry that might move me from dark to light and back again. Over and over.

Day 56

Three Decembers

Love, grace, miracles, and three Decembers.
What little bird carried the news.
No one ever knew.
When the others
were cheering them on
With a strong hand
and in the voice, they seldom heard.
—Let me see again.
Look at each other and
love my friends.
I believe
because I found shells and soft grace
I rest and instantly,
virtuously pause laughing.
Miracles and three Decembers.

Day 57

Art as healing. Today pick up a pen, pencil, crayon, and move them around a blank piece of paper. You can draw something, write words, or just let the colors liven up the page.

Day 58

Today, use a string of words to express how you are feeling. This is the start of your poem.

Day 59

Today, give your mind a rest. If you find yourself ruminating, remember that your loved one is safe and at peace and all is well.

Day 60

Today, take yourself out for ice cream. Or any other sweet treat you might like. Treat yourself.

Day 61

The Soaring Hawk

What is it about big birds that capture our attention? Here in Colorado, I have the pleasure of seeing birds of prey often. Eagles and hawks, falcons, and owls. Large and majestic. They are very confident in themselves and their place in the scheme of things. They soar free or sit perched awaiting their next meal. They hold many secrets and do not openly share. You must stop and listen.

On my earth walk, I have always been fascinated by birds. As a child, I tried to catch robins and finch as they flitted and swooped nearby. It would be quite a pleasure if one were to let me touch, hold and speak to it.

As my fascination turned to spiritual connection with the great winged creatures, I opened to their medicine and messages. Why did I find large red-tailed hawk feathers on my path? And the owl feathers. (A story devoted to owls is included in this book).

Shortly after Brandon passed hawks started to come close, visit often. At my son George's 30th birthday celebration, just three short months after Brandon's death, our entire family sat huddled together at a Rockies' baseball game. Our moods, somber. Trying our best to be happy for George. Heavy hearted. A red-tailed hawk came and circled over us. Stayed for a while. Reminded us, Brandon is here.

Today, I walked my usual route, through the park, down the winding magical path at the very place Brandon often speaks to me from spirit. I've walked this path hundreds of times and am always amazed at what I find. Today it's baby snakes flitting across the cement walkway into the early spring grass.

I moved hurriedly dance-walking to Prince's *Baby I'm a Star*. I barely noticed a colorful egg sitting upon the rock wall. Something stopped me. I had to touch this egg. Maybe a child left it. Maybe it fell from a kid's backpack on the way home from school.

I picked it up and saw it was a painted rock. Solid. Beautifully decorated. Intricate. I love rocks. I turned over the rock and it had words on it. *In loving memory of Jacob. If you find this rock, post a picture on FB.* A message of hope in grief, love in sorrow from Jacob's mom.

I tucked the rock into my pocket. I will definitely let his mom know I found this rock. Continuing my walk, I noticed two hawks following me. They circled above, slowly. Lower than usual, they flew in and out of the trees. Then they soared above. They followed me as I continued on my walk. I took off my earbuds. I listened. They were talking to each other. They flew, tails moving as if they too danced together in the sky.

Brandon and Jacob, two soaring hawks, two moms who loved them from the depths of our hearts to the heights of heaven. I contacted his mom when I returned home. She told me she too saw a hawk that day. And she lives in an entirely different state.

Thousands of miles away. The rock painter is a friend who happens to live near me.

The love of Jacob and Brandon truly does live on, and they like to let their moms know.

Day 62

Listen to some fun music today. Dance. Move your body, for it calls out to move and free the grief. Welcome in its miraculous beauty. Your body!

Day 63

Grief can be interrupted in many ways. Just for today interrupt your grief by bringing a fun memory to mind.

Day 64

Grief is an ongoing process, and you needn't be in a hurry. To slow yourself down actually helps the process move quicker. Today, slow down.

Day 65

Today be aware of your surroundings and notice the subtle. Notice the subtle blessings all around.

Day 66

Today recall a fond memory of my loved one in spirit.

Day 67

Today remember ways that you have acted on your own behalf against the grain of what you might have been taught.

How have you acted on your own behalf?

Day 68

Today walk through your day with my energy intact. Notice if you are giving too much.

Today call back your energy from all the places it lingers.

Day 69

Today give yourself a rest. Rest even if you think you could do one more thing. Especially if you are pushing yourself to do one more thing. Rest.

The True Meaning of Aloha and Ohana

Brandon's entrance into my life was an answer to a prayer. His death a devastating loss, and an opening into the realms of spirit in a more real and concise way that continues to bring me and my family great healing. The interconnectedness of life experiences, and divine interventions continue to be a vibrant part of my experience, moving me lovingly through the pain and sorrow and urging me upward on the journey of self-love and healing. I will always continue to take that next step and I will continue to ask for help along the way. And when I am asked to help another, and have the wisdom, knowledge, and energy to help, I am right there. The collective healing that ensues is miraculous. Being an answer to someone else's prayers is a blessing of courageous love in and of itself.

It was the beginning of a new decade. The 90's! I entered this decade, as a thirty-year-old new mom of four. My then husband found a new job that took us all from our home in California to a brand-new home in the state of Massachusetts. I was up for the challenge of living in a new place, but also did not know exactly what lay in store. I lived in California for twenty years, grew up there, had a big extended family and it was my home. Once I arrived, I was lost and bereft, not supported in all my life entailed but as I tend to do, I went looking for new connections and soon I met my new best friend. She too was new to the small New

England town, having moved there from Hawaii. We were two culture shocked moms. Kindred souls indeed.

We spent a lot of time together as new moms and became fast friends. She was present when Brandon was born and is Brandon's Godmother. We remain friends to this day, even though we haven't lived near each other for over thirty years. She still resides in the small New England town and me, well I moved twice since then and now make my home in Colorado.

About a year after Brandon passed, I got a frantic call from this friend who asked if I could start to pray for a Hawaiian musician. (I will call him Pu'ukani for the sake of anonymity) She told me he and his two sons just played a home concert in Boston. Heading to their next gig on the west coast, they met with a terrible fate. Wyoming winds caused a serious car accident and the tour stopped.

"Please send healing." She did not know the status of any of them, just that they were airlifted to a level one trauma center in Colorado.

My friend was a long-time member of the hula community in Massachusetts and Pu'ukani and his sons were one of their guests the week before. They were traveling the mainland on a musical tour reviving their father/sons' group with some amazing songs. They were incredibly loved, and everyone was very worried about them. She did not know much about what happened in the accident.

"Please pray for them and please find out whatever you can about their well-being."

I got on it. I put out the prayers and asked for help. I knew which level one trauma center they must have been taken to, because I live near the only one in a five-hundred-mile radius of interstate 80. The Wyoming border is close, and I know well the treacherous winds and weather on the Wyoming highways. I put out all my feelers and tried to find out anything I could about the father and sons. I was called to help by my good friend, Brandon, and the ancestors of this beautiful Hawaiian man.

I prayed and meditated for this man and his children, whom I had never met. I could feel the spirit so strong. I received a powerful vision of large green mountains and many Hawaiian holy people praying and chanting. They told me the Musician was gravely ill, and they, his ancestors were gathered to help him heal or return to them. It was not yet clear as to which. I asked them to use me and guide me to how I might best help. It was an incredibly powerful vision, and I was/am so very honored that I was called to assist.

I was however having trouble finding him on the earthbound level, for he was not registered as a patient at the hospital. I went through all the channels I knew to find him. I also followed all the protocol for privacy and asked for divine intervention every step of the way. I went on social media and found the information I needed. His sons were unscathed. Pu'ukani was not. He suffered severe trauma and was in a coma. His entire family flew in from Hawaii and was holding vigil by his side.

I was finally able to connect with his brother, who was so very receptive and thanked me profusely for finding them. It was confirmed that Pu'ukani was registered at the Level One Trauma center near me. He was registered under his English name and that is why I could not find him. *This is the same hospital that Brandon's good friend Miguel (from the story on Day 90) stayed in just a few weeks prior. Same floor, and eventually the same room.

His brother invited me to the hospital that day. It was as if they knew me already, for I was greeted with hugs from the big extended family. They called me Auntie, and this is when I was introduced to the word Ohana. It means family but it is more than that. It is the essence of what it means to be safe and connected to others in a way that we know that we are all taking care of each other. I knew I was a vital part of a divinely guided intervention to help them through a most traumatic time.

The prognosis for Pu'ukani was not good but his parents would never give up hope. His brother told me I was a godsend because they were all going to have to leave soon, and his mother would be staying alone by his brother's side, tending to him as he barely held onto life. I assured Pu'kani's brother that I would stay with his mother. I completely understood this mother's intense love and need to help her son recover. I would be her friend and companion to help her navigate what lay ahead. I knew this area, this was my community, for it was my home for 18 years. I lived a few miles from the hospital and would make myself available.

He told me, "you are Ohana". I nodded my head and asked myself, how it was that they trusted me. I then remembered my vision with the Hawaiian ancestors. I trusted they had this already figured out. Probably even before I was born!

His brother took me to Pu'ukani's hospital room, and I entered tentatively. His mom greeted me with a warm hug. She was like a beautiful Hawaiian goddess sitting in a cold intensive care unit in a hard plastic chair up against a big window overlooking the harsh ruggedness of the Colorado Rocky Mountains in the barren brown of summer. She donned a flower in her hair and a big smile. She thanked me for coming and asked how I knew of her son. I told her, my dear friend told me to come. She nodded and welcomed me by the bedside of her child. A grown man on the brink of death. A mother refusing to give up. I understood.

I sat close holding her hand. I listened to her tell of her will to will her son to live. His brother gave me the full scope of the severity of Pu'ukani's injuries. He was without oxygen for a long while. His brain registered permanent damage. He was in an induced coma and could not breathe on his own. Their Aloha spirit and the sheer strength of his mother and father refusing to give in to anything but complete healing kept them all going.

"The doctors wanted us to take him off life support. My husband and I said no. We know he is in there and he will get better." She commented with fierce mother courage. I nodded and held her hand.

I glanced at Pu'ukani, a handsome, large forty-something man, laying as still as could be, with tubes and machines connected to all sorts of places keeping his traumatized body alive. I was no stranger to intensive care and the hope and terror that fill the moments in between the machine's constant beeps. On the brink of life and death with only the will of a love so strong keeping him from teetering on this side of the portal. She urged me to talk to him, to touch his hand if I wished. I walked to his side, and as I went to lay my hand upon his I was shocked. His arms bore the markings of Hawaiian tribal tattoos that looked exactly like the ones from my dream of the Gifts from the Brown Bear. (story on Day 79).

I was in another portal of divine intervention, a place in time where once again I was lifted up into the miracle of the moment. I was in awe. I thanked my angels and the divine, and as if the angels of healing answered me, my freshwater pearl necklace fell from my neck and onto the ground next to his bed.

I stayed by Pu'ukani's mother's side late into that day and each day forward for several months. I prayed, shared Reiki, even helped find the best rehab center when the time came. I met a few of his close friends who are still my friends today, as one by one they came to visit. I did not share my story of great loss with her, instead I held healing space for this mother whose son would live and eventually recover. It was a long miraculous road. She played his music for him on constant loop on an old cd boombox someone brought in. She gave every medical professional that tended to her son copies of his music cd's. He awoke from the coma and his brain healed slowly. He had to learn to eat and talk and walk. He had to learn to use his arms and legs again. A man pronounced brain dead came back. The issues that remain affect his eyesight, and he is still recovering the full use of his body. He is sharing his story now too. A miraculous recovery with many angels of many varieties.

Through it all, many small miracles occurred, as is the way when divine intervention is at play. The divine life force connected me with others on this similar journey. The divine life force connected me with the Hawaiian Ancestors of whom I never would have met, lest the path of my life took me to this exact place at this exact time. The power of trust in the bigger scheme of things, grew immensely, and while things may not have turned out as I would wish them for myself and my youngest son, the power and potency of love lives on across time and space, earth, and heaven. A benevolent and helpful source connects us all. This source is a healing source.

Through it all, I became enveloped in Ohana, the power of family. Not only blood family, but those who are there for you more deeply and profoundly than any family of blood may be. Soul family. What I did not learn, nor receive from my family of origin, I received unconditionally from this Ohana. They were there for me, as I for them. In a few short months we became bonded for life. I learned of Aloha. The power of love, affection, generosity, speaking from the heart, patience and listening. 'Lo means to share, and 'ha' is the breath of life or life force energy. What a glorious and most perfect energy to live in and wish upon others many times every day!

Brandon led me to this Ohana, through my dear friend, his godmother. Brandon lived the spirit of Aloha in his short life. I received so much healing as I accompanied my new Ohana through some of the most heroic days of their lives. It was three months later that my friends left Colorado and went back home to Hawaii. He was healed enough to travel and received enough rehabilitation that he was on his way.

A few weeks before he was well enough to travel, I drove his father to the airport. His father gave me a Hawaiian name- 'Anela'.

"You are our angel. Anele means angel."

"Well, that is quite a compliment." I said. "I am guided by angels, that is for sure."

His father then told me the story of his ancestors. They come from a line of Hawaiian cowboys. They live and work on the land in Kona for generations. At the turn of the twentieth century his great grandfathers and uncles came right here to Colorado/Wyoming and competed in a national rodeo. He told me his ancestors won many of the competitions and showed those mainland cowboys up. They were not treated well; racism was in full force. They were looked down upon, being they were indigenous peoples from an island far away. I was told it was Teddy Roosevelt who insisted the best darn cowboys (Hawaiian cowboys) on the planet must be allowed to compete in the National rodeo so very long ago. None of his family had come back to Colorado for a hundred years, but there was something about this place, he said.

I see it this way; here it was over one hundred years later, and their great-great-grandson lay dying in a field in Wyoming. They came to his rescue, and called on all who would listen. Brandon, me, my bestie, and all the Ohana who carry Aloha in their hearts and live it every day. That is how divine interventions happen.

Day 71

Today as you walk, remember that with each step you are receiving healing love into the soles of your feet.

Each step is a healing. If you are unable to walk, please know that the essence of the earth comes up to greet you today. In whatever way you need it most.

Day 72

Today reflect on family. Who are the people in your soul family?

Day 73

Today imagine that you have benevolent ancestors.

You may not know who they are. They may have lived a few generations back. There is the love of an ancestor just waiting for your acknowledgment. You will feel this today.

Day 74

Today imagine your ancestors of the future. Send them love.

Day 75

Today feel yourself a part of the past and the future. Today, receive healing love from all areas of time.

Day 76

Today use the healing power of nature. Find a tree and hug it. If you are not comfortable hugging, a smile will do.

Day 77

Today take a leap of faith. Try something new. Do something out of the ordinary and reap the benefits.

Day 78

Today list the top three things that make you feel better. I invite you to do one of those things today.

The Gifts from the Brown Bear Dream

The Dream: I was sitting on a folding chair in an empty room. A great brown bear came to me and lay its head across my feet. His mouth on my right foot. He lay this way for just a few moments. Then as quick as he came over to me, he got up and left. I was not afraid during this visit from the bear, and I felt no pain. But somehow, I knew the bear had bit my right foot. I looked down at my foot and sure enough, it was mangled and bloody. Again, I was not afraid or in any pain. I was curious. A man then came over to me, as I still sat in the chair. He told me he was a doctor and would tend to me. He examined my foot. Still, it did not cause pain. He pulled out something and handed it to me.

"The bear left you a tooth."

I took it in the palm of my hand and studied it. It did not look like a tooth, instead it looked to be a small talisman with black markings very similar to the tribal markings of the Hawaiian or Minoan tribes. (These markings are also on a rain stick Brandon gave me for my birthday one year. This rain stick stands next to his urn. I did not however make this connection until much later in my waking world.)

I thought this was a most spectacular gift. "I shall put this on my altar." I told the doctor.

The doctor continued to tend to my foot. He inserted a long wire to measure the depth of the wound. After a while, he spoke.

"The wound is deep, but it will heal."

An outpouring of truth ran through my body. A rush of knowing, and acknowledgment. All the pain and suffering was indeed deep, but I was reassured that I would heal. I was filled with a hope.

The Doctor then said. "The Bear left you another gift. A claw. Let me get it for you." Then I awoke.

This dream itself was so very healing. I was reassured on a level that touched my soul. This dream held much for me and resonated deeply. I felt assured that the pain associated with my family of origin would heal. I felt assured that the pain associated with the death of Brandon would heal. The bear came to let me know that in the deepest wound, is found the healing. Messages through my nighttime dreams, talismans, bear medicine, a healer. My pain was not for naught. I received a great healing in that dream. One that spurred me to continue my journey.

I wrote the poem found on Day 80. I made an art piece that hangs in my healing room. The piece depicts my great brown bear coming through the portal of 111. The bear is flanked by two ancient Yew trees in the place of angels. And it was a few months after this dream that I would meet the Hawaiian musician and see the same tribal markings on his arm that were on my bear tooth in this dream. The wound is indeed deep. And I will heal. And so will you.

Day 80

Following the Path of Love

I followed the path of love

around and around, up and out.

A gracious growl, a ferocious fire

a torrid rain

a gentle pond.

Surrender, release

Hold on, let go.

Up, down

within and through

Claw and tooth.

Medicine of the Ages

the Healing continues.

Day 81

Making Sacred the Land

It was a balmy April day a mere three months after Brandon's death. That day I was feeling intensely paralyzing emotional pain. I was inconsolable. I needed something to help move this pain. During the first weeks and months I found it imperative for me to use my voice to move the pain through by moaning and screaming. The primal release was uncontrollable and necessary. After a while I started to figure out what I needed and would support myself in crying or writing or screaming out. The pain came in bursts, much like labor pains. This day was different. I needed something different. Labor pains with no baby at the end. Labor pains with only the pain.

I spoke on the phone with my friend, and I shared my pain. I cried. Something I did not let myself do very often because I was never safe in relationships to cry or ask for my needs to be met. I needed the safety of my own growing self-compassion and maybe I would take a chance with her. As I cried to her, I heard myself say exactly what I needed.

"I need to go to the place where my son took his last breath. I need to go to the site of the car accident."

Yes, my soul and spirit were there with him on that fateful day, but I was not there physically while he took his last breath. I could not comfort him then, and I desperately needed to do something to counter this fact. This was a very big deal because I knew it would open a slew of incredibly uncomfortable feelings, but I had to do it.

I packed snacks, crystals, oils, and some special talismans. I looked at his death certificate to get the coordinates. Looking at his death certificate brought a whole other level of grief up. It is horrific to see in writing the time, date and cause of my child's death. I cherish the birth certificates of my children. I still hold each of my five grown children's certificates of birth, in a fireproof box in my home. And Brandon's death certificate. No one warned me how it would feel to hold a death certificate. See the formality and finality of it all in a legal document. How do you read those words without crying out in pain? I added this feat to the day's need for healing and drove the seventy miles to find the exact spot where his car landed and he took his last breath. The directions were not as clear as I'd hoped, but I used my intuition. I sat on one side of the street where I thought the accident occurred. I sat for a while and then realized this did not feel right. I then looked across the street and saw a most magnificent sight. An eagle soaring. I followed the eagle and found myself in a very small tucked away park. The park is called Flyin'B. It was beautiful. A historic landmark that would never be built over. I looked around the park and kept feeling Brandon's presence. I heard him ask, "Mom, isn't this beautiful?"

I had to agree. "Yes, Brandon. Big trees, a pond, and a walking trail. It was indeed beautiful and perfect." Very similar to my neighborhood park where I took daily walks. My park and this park both had a pond and beautiful tall trees.

"If you had to go, I thank you for picking a beautiful place." I answered.

Once again, I was drawn into the continuous synchronicities of divine intervention. The look and feel of this park, and the name too. One of Brandon's nicknames is 'B'. Flying B is appropriate. He loved to fly, go fast, skateboard and get air. His death certificate did use the verbiage that his car flew 120 feet in the air before landing in a retention pond. A knowing of the greater scheme of things held me tight as these details, as sordid as could be, seemed to make a sort of sense. I could not stop his soul from doing what he needed, but in this great and tragic loss, he once again made sure I had exactly what I would need. To know his spirit flew home, and to know he exited in a most beautiful place. The beauty and power of nature was staring me in the face. I was held in this healing love.

I walked the park and sat for a while, but I knew this was not the exact spot. The car was found in a very small retention pond area, where was that? The water was shallow and barely visible tucked in an open space with a railing and a cement drainage container. Again, the eagle soared, and I followed it a very short way down the street to the exact spot. There it was. I saw the tracks where they pulled his car from the ditch. I called in my angels and the divine mother. I called in all my spirit helpers and Brandon's. I walked the whole area. A wide area of about 100 feet in each direction. I placed a crystal in the shallow water of the retention pond and made sacred this land on which my son took his last breath. It was now and will always be Holy Land. I placed flowers and took a rock and a bit of the water. I did my cleansing, clearing and used all that I learned and knew from my ancestors past. This is what mothers have been doing since the beginning of time. I knew to make this place into hallowed ground.

I left more healed, and today I return to this place when called. On the first anniversary of his passing my grandson found the crystal I placed in the water that April day nine months prior. It washed up many feet away from any water's edge. The quiet, dark road is now built up and there are streetlights to find the way and to give light to anyone who would ever happen to fly off the road. No one else will suffer the same fate my son did when the road was dark, and his car could not be found. The Flyin'B park will always be there, and the retention pond area too, for it is holy ground, now and forever.

Day 82

What does making sacred mean to you? Today make sacred something you value.

Day 83

Today, tend to your feelings by writing down each one on a slip of paper. Then put them into a jar or box. Label the jar or box, Sacred Emotions.

Day 84

Today, create an altar. An altar is made by placing some special items on a table or dresser. These items remind you that your life is sacred. Place the container of Sacred Emotions upon the altar.

Day 85

Today is about feeling safe. Grieving requires a level of emotional safety.

Day 86

Today pay attention to the symbols known as numbers. What numbers are you seeing a lot of? Any patterns? Just notice.

Day 87

Today let yourself feel without fearing judgment from self or others.

Day 88

Today practice taking advantage of whatever the weather brings. What is the literal weather today? Take advantage of it in a way that brings you a smile.

Day 89

Today remember your connection with that which is lasting and nourishing. What is something that has stood the test of time?

Day 90

Brandon Is My Angel

Brandon always drew people to him. His friendly manner, warm smile and adventurous spirit flowed freely since he entered this life. Children and adults were drawn to his authentic, playful, and caring charm. He had many friends, loved to explore, hang out and have a good time. If you were his friend, so were your family members. If you were Brandon's friends, I was their mom too, and his siblings theirs. I did not know the extent of his strong connection with so many people until experiencing the many divine interventions after his untimely death. I did not know how much he meant to so many people. I did not know exactly how he was able to love and be loved in ways that defied time and space. One family in particular consisting of three sons and their hard-working mama became a part of Brandon's divine intervention schemes. The extent of which is filled with healing miracles, divine timing, and the presence of angels.

It was about a year after Brandon's passing. My son George texted me that *Miguel, the youngest of the three brothers, was in a serious car accident. He was taken to the nearby level one trauma center with injuries requiring immediate lifesaving surgeries.

"His family could really use your support, Mom. Especially his mom." George told me.

"And Mom, Miguel said something about seeing Brandon during the accident."

I would gladly go to the hospital and offer my support. When I arrived, I found his family sitting pensively in the waiting room. I was a bit uncomfortable, for I only met his mom once before and I didn't want to intrude. They welcomed me with open arms, as if they expected me, and I learned part of what happened.

Miguel was driving very early in the morning to get to work. He was involved in a head on collision on a two-lane highway. (I would later learn that the crash site was right outside the event center where we held Brandon's celebration of life.) Unfortunately, the other driver did not make it. Apparently neither of them were wearing a seatbelt. In the crash, Miguel ended up in the back of his truck pinned down and sustaining many serious injuries. When the paramedics found him, he was telling them, "I have to tell Brandon's mom, I have to tell Brandon's dad! I saw Brandon!".

The paramedics and ER staff didn't know what he meant, but word spread, and my son George was told to call me and have me come to be with the family while they awaited Miguel's surgeries and recovery. I felt Brandon's familiar desire to help in any way he could and his urging that I help now. I sat with the family for the next several days as Miguel recuperated. The hospital room stay, the family gathering, the prayers, the comforts, I knew this well. I was in service to the family for a few weeks as Miguel started to heal from his injuries. His leg was crushed, and he would need extensive physical therapy, but all his other injuries would heal. A miracle!

I sat with this wonderful family and learned stories about Brandon I never would have known. The stories delightful and healing to hear. I learned he would go over to their house when the sons weren't home, just to hang with his mom and have her cook him noodles and eggs! That was Brandon.

I shared my faith with the family. The faith that our soul lives on! Somehow, they found great comfort in my presence. It was as if Brandon sent me to them to add my comfort as only I could. I was his ambassador of good will and healing energy. I didn't dare ask about what Miguel had to tell me about Brandon until it was the right time. I have come to understand that many divine interventions are difficult to put into words. They are held inside your heart and mind as healing balms. Often wrapped in trauma they are not always necessary to relive but will change you forever.

Finally, after a few weeks he was well enough, and we had a few moments alone in his hospital room. He shared with me what happened when the accident occurred, and Brandon appeared. He did not remember much of the accident, but he does remember waking up in the back of the truck in a lot of pain. He was scared and truly thought he was dying. Then, a big light appeared, and he heard Brandon's voice. He then saw Brandon, and as plain as day Brandon said to Miguel, "don't worry, it's not your time" and then he was gone, and the paramedics arrived. Miguel told me Brandon is his guardian angel. He kept a photo of Brandon (since his passing) on his visor along with the Saints and Our Lady Of Guadalupe. He says Brandon helped him that day and he will continue to thank him and carry him with him wherever he goes.

I gave the family a few sets of rosary beads to take with them when they travel. I know Brandon continues his friendships by watching out for his buddies from the other realms. He is indeed an angel to many.

Day 91

Today is a day to call to mind friendship. Who is the friend that is there for you during the most trying of times?

Day 92

Friends can show up when we need them most. Today you are a friend to yourself. What would your friend do for you today. Do that.

Day 93

Today spend time in nature. What places are healing for you in nature? Have you discovered a new healing place in nature? Imagine that the energy of the place called you there. Imagine that the wildlife, and the plants all welcome you.

Day 94

Today talk with someone who will just listen. Give yourself the gift of a good listener.

Day 95

Today put down a burden. Leave it down all day.

Day 96

Today is a day for play. Today is the day to do something fun, just because.

Day 97

Today do not answer any questions. Especially the ones that come into your mind that have no answers.

Day 98

Today lovingly imagine that you are surrounded by a bubble of protective love. Use this as a boundary as often as needed.

Day 99

Today spend time in solitude. Remember that your loved one is always nearby. You are never truly alone. Love is always near.

Day 100

One Year

It was coming up on the one-year anniversary of Brandon's death. A surge of dread coursed through me and met me with every thought. So very many questions tumbled around in my still grieving, traumatized mind. I didn't want it to be a year since I last saw my son. How could it be one year already? It went so fast, and yet it was all so painfully slow. How could I possibly honor such a horrific and tragic day? How could I not? After all it was still my duty as his mother to do so. In steps my grief counselor. She gently reminded me that I could plan for what I needed. And most of all, I learned that I needed time to decide and choose. There was no rushing in grief. I remembered the vow I made. I would learn how to walk through grieving and bereavement and I would heal. This vow gave me just the right amount of energy I needed to meet the one-year anniversary of Brandon's physical death with great self-care, self-love, compassion, and healing.

My grief counselor asked me questions and gave me lots of space to find the answers. Again, there is no right or wrong way to meet yourself in grief. But the questions helped. What might I need as the day approached? How might I ritualize this day in sacred reverence? She knew me by now and knew ritual helped me so much. Given the healing space to feel and to choose what is best for me, I once again made a plan. What I found out was that it was the time leading up to this day that was truly the hardest. It was the dread and fear of the unknown. The planning was helpful. It gave me back a sort of control. I could honor my son's life and my own need for compassionate healing.

I decided I would go to the site of the crash. I knew it now to be a holy place since I went and cleared the land in April. I shared my plans with my children, but I did so with the caveat that we were each free to do something different when the day arrived. I knew each of my children grieved and honored the passing of their brother differently.

When the day came, I traveled the seventy-five miles to the site of the car accident. It was a beautiful sunny January day. There was no snow on the ground. When I arrived, I walked towards the place and was met by my son and daughter in love and their two little ones. They brought balloons and flowers and wish paper. I was so very happy to see them. Then, up drove another car and out came a young woman and her little child. The woman carried a large wreath. I did not know her. She asked if I was Brandon's mother. I was suddenly very protective of this day, and all it held. I asked her who she was and why she was there. She gently answered.

"I worked with Brandon for quite a while at the health club. My daughter and I made this wreath for him. He was a very special person to me, and I wanted to honor him. Is it ok if I leave this with you?"

Divine Intervention. A blessing indeed. A stranger with such love for my son. She placed the wreath where I asked her to and left, thanking me for allowing her to give this present to me in honor of Brandon. I felt her respect as a gift from Brandon.

One of my little grandsons and I decided to walk the perimeter of the retention pond area. I knew we would find something that Brandon left. We sure did! There were feathers galore. So many that I exclaimed!

"Rocco, we found the Mother Lode."

"What's the Mother Lode, Gma?" he asked in his little seven-year-old inquisitive way.

"It means that this is where we found the gold. A lot of feathers!" I answered.

Yes, a lot. We wrote on the wish paper, sending our wishes out into the Universe. We laid on the ground, backs supported by the hard earth, watching as we let four balloons go. I know balloons are not good for our atmosphere yet seeing the balloons dance and float for a good long time, was amazingly magical. We all watched for a long while as the last of the balloons were out of sight. I felt our hearts expand out into the Universe, connecting with the spheres of where Brandon could now travel without a problem.

We left the flowers and crystals near the water where the car landed. My grandson found the crystal I placed in the water many months earlier. I found a large piece of the Maserati laying amidst the winter grass. It was a piece of the center console with the emblem of the Maserati, a trident. A powerful icon of the God

Neptune and of the sea. How did I miss this the first time? Well, it would not stay here, I would take it with. After all, this is now the place my son flew home to heaven!

I ended the day going to my eldest son's home. They took such good care of me. He held me as I wept. We all healed a bit deeper that day, with Brandon divinely intervening to be sure I was held in the most love possible. I felt it so.

Every single step I took to support myself and my family through the unknown territory of grief, bereavement and mourning resulted in leading me to a place where I could stand on the place my son perished and feel his essence of pure love all around. I could look into my eldest son's eyes, my daughter in love's eyes and feel the most love and care imaginable. I could take my little grandson's hands and we could traverse the grounds where his uncle died and find magical feathers and heart shaped rocks, left for us to find. I could receive a gift of pure thoughtful love from a friend who thought of my son that day.

One step each day added up to 365 days of a bereaved mom knowing without a doubt, her son lived on in so many divinely intervening moments.

Day 101

Counting the days is a way to honor how far you have come. How might you honor how far you have come? Do something generous for yourself today.

Day 102

Today, believe in angels. What might an angel on earth look like? You will meet one today.

Day 103

Today remember that grieving has no timeline. Take as long as needed.

Day 104

Today bring to mind community. What and who makes up your community now? Greif requires a certain kind of community. If you have a different community now than before your loss, fear not. This new community is here for you.

Day 105

What gives meaning to your life? What matters to you?

Day 106

Great loss makes all that is unimportant seem even more unimportant. Over one year's time life has cleared out frivolous, unimportant activities and worries.

What is no longer important?

Day 107

What is most important to you now? Today, remind yourself of that which matters?

Day 108

Today spend time with someone you love. This someone can even be YOU. Walking yourself through loss, transition and new beginnings is the most loving thing you can do.

Day 109

Today, write a thank you note to yourself for all you have done to help your life be a bit better.

Day 110

What might it be like to live a healing life after tragic loss?

Today believe in the possibility of living a healing life.

Day 111

Seven Years of Recovery

I view the hours, days, weeks, months, and years post death of my youngest child as a recovery period. I spent this most sacred time, recovering the shattered pieces of my heart, recovering a way to make sense of the senseless tragedy and loss, recovering my soul, recovering moments of healing, recovering emotional health and stability amidst deep sorrow and loss. I honor my son's life and my own by recovering all the parts of me that were dismissed and disowned from the times before his death. I recover all the experiences that I lived through and now I focus on continuing to build a life of real, true, viable love. January 13, 2024, marks seven years.

On this day, I enter a new time period and a new cycle and into this new space, I bring the past seven years of recovery. I name the new cycle, 'a lived miracle'. The creations of my heart formed into sustainable, viable, tangible experiences. These creations came from a compilation of the minutes, hours, days, weeks, lived and the way I lived them. Recovery time is most valuable.

My creations include my home, my work, my writings, and stories. My creations include my relationships with others and most especially with my children and grandchildren. Within these creations came a new grandchild. She arrived February 22, 2024. She is the first grandchild born since Brandon went through the portal. (If you read the miracle of *"What Happened When I Died"* you will remember the date of February 22 as a special day). This little miracle babe is the first child of my miracle child George, who was born 37 years ago with a heart issue of the most serious sort. Their lives are both miracles. Her presence is a miracle of love that includes George, his wife, Raeden, and all the divine interventions that played a part in seeing this little one into being. A lived miracle.

I step into this new cycle with all the synchronicities, wisdom, guidance, blessings, and healing surrounding and uplifting me. On the 7th anniversary of Brandon's passing, I experienced a divine intervention that showed me that a tender new beginning has indeed commenced. The story is as follows~

On January 22, 2017, after Brandon's celebration of life, friends and family gathered at my home. The crowd was wearing on me. I needed some escape for a moment and stepped outside to see what might be happening in the night sky in my small, quiet suburban neighborhood. There at the end of my driveway I found my kids, along with friends and various family members huddled in the chill night air, chatting, smoking, crying, hugging, and laughing. A group of my beloveds gathering outside under the light of the exceptionally bright waning crescent moon with the pain of death heavy in our midst. We were trying to find some comfort in the world that precariously turned on its side a few short days ago.

My daughter in love started howling at the moon. I joined in, as did others. Immediately the streetlight directly across from my home flashed on and off! We all knew it was the doing of Brandon. We laughed and cried and continued our howls.

For the next two years, that exact streetlight continued to go on and off on cue. It is directly in front of my home, and I can see it from every window on the front of my house. I would ask Brandon in my mind to please show me he is here, and it would immediately flash. When my kids pulled up to my home or I walked outside it would flash. It felt like a constant hello from Brandon. My little grandsons loved this miracle. They would sit outside on the driveway, and we would ask Brandon to show us he was here. Without hesitation, the light would flash. It brought us all great comfort and undeniable knowing of Brandon's continued presence. After about two years as magically as it started, it stopped. Brandon was very present in so many other ways and continues to be so, and the ceasing of the flashing streetlight seemed a natural progression of him moving on to bigger and better feats. There was no physical explanation for the stopping, no streetlight repair, just Brandon's energy flowing through to let us know he lived on.

On September 25, 2023, on his thirty-first heavenly birthday, I went outside and looked at the streetlight. I asked him for old time's sake to make it flash. It did not. I was however compelled to walk a bit farther down the block and into the open field across the street, all to get a better look at the rising full harvest moon. It was gorgeous, alive, and so bright. I turned to look in the direction of the streetlight and there in the west sky, just above the rooftops and streetlight was a brilliant display of fireworks. I stood watching the moon rising in the east and the fireworks showing off in the west. What a gift. I knew it was from Brandon.

One hundred and eleven days later, (111) on the seven-year anniversary of his passing the streetlight did indeed start flashing off and on. I saw it from my living room window and could not believe my eyes. And yes, it did so on cue. It continued for a few days. Then a city repair crew showed up, they replaced the light with a new and different type of streetlight.

I felt a deep resolve and completion as I watched them remove the old lamp. Something different is being asked of me now. Not a moving on, or forgetting, or closure. There will never be any moving on, forgetting or closure. This is harmful to imagine, yet it is often an uttered phrase from unconscious people. I have learned that many people are very uncomfortable with death and will do anything to pretend it either does not happen, does not affect them or will even shame those of us who are deep in the throes of grief. I am here to counter this and offer deeply compassionate love in the times of grief.

Truth is, there is a "moving with" and an opening of the portal of divine interventions and a remembering of the truth that love lives on and never dies. In the seven year stretch of time my son in spirit and I created new bonds. Grief lessens, and this experience of loss is a part of the dynamic and beautiful mosaic of my life. I tended to my needs with patience, humor, and deepening self-compassion. He was always there when I needed him with his part in the divine interventions and will continue to be a part of my life always.

I know in the depth of my bones that it is time to take the seven years of recovery and give myself grace to settle into my life and all that I have now. I take every moment with me, for the most painful moments have been transmuted by the way I met myself in the deepest pain and how I live my life in honor of my experiences and challenges. I live onward within a life that suits me with a continuing allowance of healing love on order every single day. I live in an expansive way, like a spiral moving ever within and without with each breath I take. A full circle that never stops, just keeps moving upward and includes all that I am. The questions I now ask for this new season, cycle and new life are different questions.

What might it feel like to live fully immersed in my own life, living fully in my own experiences? What does it mean to me to be living my own deeply meaningful experiences out loud and fully? How can I best support myself to continue to live a life that includes great tragedy and loss, trauma and pain, AND great healing, love, new life, and joy? How might I share this with others who have experienced the unimaginable?

Perhaps you might start by asking yourself, how might your life be changed if you dare to imagine a healing so deep and powerful that it defies time and space? How might you live if you see all the divine interventions that have been appearing all along? How might you live if you knew the entire universe and your soul was conspiring on your behalf?

We are a part of every divine intervention we encounter. We each play a part in divine interventions that include others. To live life as if it were a miracle opens you to the truth that you are so much more than your physical being. You are an angel on earth, you are a being of love. You never know how your existence changes the course of another's life for the better, or they change yours. It is a true miracle to awaken to the truth that we are all a part of the divine interventions that make this world a place where healing happens and love lives on. My prayer for you is that you know yourself to be a divinely inspired part of the miracles of life that occur each and every day.

Resources

Heart of Gaia Creative Healing Arts, my healing arts practice, offers grief support through Reiki, Spiritual Counsel, Mediumship, guidance for Ceremony and Ritual, journaling through grief and Spiritual Connection Groups. In person and virtual. www.marydagostino.com

In loving memory of my child Brandon, I created Brandon's Angels, a non-profit organization that provides care packages and resources for those who are experiencing a death loss. www.brandonsangels.com

If you have a divine intervention that you would like to share, I would love to hear about it. Contact me at mary@marydagostino.com

I recommend trained and licensed grief therapy. Remember grieving is not an illness. Psychology Today is a good resource. Grief therapy, group art therapy, music, and journaling with those who know how to hold and create sacred space for the griever's heart is what I recommend. Body work, Reiki, cranial sacral and massage. Be sure to find someone who is trauma informed and can hold your grief in tender loving care.

Podcasts to support you: Grief and Rebirth https://ireneweinberg.com/

Sandra Champlain's Shades of the Afterlife and We Don't Die Radio

Books: Good to the Last Drop, Embracing Your Life's Third Chapter https://a.co/d/07zK2qT7

Soul Signs by Shirley A. Lyster https://a.co/d/094Smcd5

Mary D'Agostino is mom to five grown children and grandmother to seven. She is an author, artist, healer, astrologer, diviner, soul medium and creator of Heart of Gaia Creative Healing Arts. She offers her home and heart as a healing balm in service to healing love. Her offerings may be found at her website www.marydagostino.com

Mary makes her home right up against the foothills of the Northern Colorado Rockies where each day holds the magnificence and beauty of this fleeting life on Earth. Please visit Brandon's Angels to find out how you can be assisted in your grief loss or help another. www.brandonsangels.com

Brandon loving Life.

Made in the USA
Middletown, DE
12 December 2024

66783588R00099